TUE THANK YOU!

Dreaming BIG and Small

NEW AND COLLECTED POEMS BY

SARA HOLBROOK AND MICHAEL SALINGER

ARTWORK BY

SCOTT PICKERING

StreamlinePUBLISHING

Dreaming BIG and Small

ISBN 978-1-7325191-2-1
Library of Congress Control Number: 2019900306

First Paperback Edition
The text of this book is set in FreightSans.

9 8 7 6 5 4 3 2 1

Printed in the United States of America.

Why, William, on the old grey stone,

Thus for length of half a day,

Why, William, sit you thus alone,

And dream your time away? ...

William Wordsworth

To Jane Yolen, a continuing inspiration. Thanks for your sage guidance through critical passages. – SH

To my sons Frank and Max, two excellent men who turned out better than I could have dreamed. – MS

To my mom & dad - Audrey & Art Pickering for always encouraging me to follow my whacky dreams in this adventure called "life." I love you. – SP

How this book was born:

Typically, poets write poems for publication and then the publisher turns them over to an artist to illustrate. Most times, the poet doesn't even get to talk to the artist, which makes the big reveal exciting to the writer. Roughly a gazillion books (by exact count) have been created that way.

But who wants to be just typical?

This time, instead of turning over a stack of poems to Scott to illustrate, Sara and Michael mined his Instagram account and chose images to illustrate with words. What attracted them to his artwork is that it is definitely not typical. Some poems were written for a specific piece of artwork (ekphrastic poems), and some came from their archives of previously written, anthologized or out-of-print poems. A few of the artistic images Scott created to go with specific poems, but mostly we worked the other way around.

Michael and Sara hope this book inspires you to write poetry about images you find or create in your head. *Note: if you find them, be sure you have the permission of the artist or photographer before sharing the images!* Scott hopes his artwork inspires you to never be satisfied with typical.

This book is a true creative collaboration: writers and artist. Michael and Sara are poets who are friends with artist Scott Pickering in their hometown of Cleveland, OH.

ekphrastic poetry: "Ekphrastic poems focus on works of art—usually paintings, photographs, or statues. And modern ekphrastic poems have generally shrugged off antiquity's obsession with elaborate description, and instead have tried to interpret, inhabit, confront, and speak to their subjects." (Academy of American Poets, www.poets.org)

Table of Contents

Dreaming

Dreaming BIG and Small

by Michael Salinger and Sara Holbrook

Back flips.
A solo act.
Flying high.
Barefoot grass.
Waffles with syrup.
My name on a star.
A new box of crayons.
An avatar.
A standing O.
The winning goal.
10,000 likes.
A fishing pole.
Anything with sprinkles.

Counting clouds,
atop this wall.
Wings spread wide,
dreaming
BIG
and
small.

When the Wind Blows

by Michael Salinger

When the wind blows right
on a clear, cool
end-of-summer night,
trains that are really
miles away
sound like they are
just outside my window.
The whistle blast,
and the steel wheels clack,
ride through the air
as if their track
ran straight and smooth,
just outside my window.
Then the sound seems to fade
as it follows the train
to wherever it's going,
and I fall asleep
in my warm bed knowing
that the world rolls on,
just outside my window.

My Dreams

by Sara Holbrook

Open
window by my bed,
the EXIT
for my dreams.
Among the light-lured bugs,
mobbed against the screen,
my dreams
step out at night,
stretch,
and vanish
out of sight.

Up

by Michael Salinger

Where does the sky begin?
I mean,
what do you call the air a half inch
above a blade of grass?
What is the force which creates wind?
Which kind of clouds hold rain?
How can air be thin?
How far up does oxygen exist?
Where does all that blue come from?
And why is it colder higher up
when you're actually closer to the sun?

Elation

by Sara Holbrook

Elation
appears
without foundation
and practical ties.
All-you-want,
FREE BALLOONS!
Primary thoughts
that swell
up, up
my insides.
Jump and reach!
We're on the rise –
yellow, green, red –
against
azure skies.

Horrific

by Michael Salinger

Horrific will make you holler!
Not with joy, but with blood-freezing fear.
He's a hundred times worse than scary.
Shocking, revolting, and dreadfully frightful,
Horrific finds everything awful, delightful.
Horrific makes your neck hair hop,
your stomach flip, flop and drop.
Your heart will bounce inside your chest.
He won't give you a rest.
He'll dare you to not make a sound.
Watch out!
It's horrific!
And he's not messing around.

Gruesome

by Michael Salinger

Gruesome is kind of hard to look at
because he is not the prettiest sight.
His appearance could make your mother
gasp, groan and shudder in fright.
An eyeball dangling out of its socket.
Intestines outside instead of in.
Body parts strewn across a room.
Maggots crawling out of the skin.
His flesh is peeling off his bones.
His hair is full of worms.
He takes you out of your comfort zone.
He's gonna make you squirm.

Puzzled

by Sara Holbrook

Bewildered.
Stumped.
Messed up.
Lost.
Gob smacked.
In doubt.
Perplexed.
Baffled.
Befuddled.
Stuck.
At a loss.
Clueless.
Confused.
Uncertain.
What's next?

Two Wheels That Go Around

by Michael Salinger

Two wheels that go around.
Two pedals for my feet.
Two handles on a bar.
One chain.
One seat.
One bell to let you know
I am coming up fast
Ring, ring, ring, ring, ring.
Watch out
while I pass!

When I Ride my Bike

by Michael Salinger

I'm streaking like a lightning bolt.
My helmet's hard as a turtle shell.
I balance like an acrobat.
Watch out! When I hit the bell.
My wheels whirl like a windmill.
I corner like a racing car,
braking quick as a light switch flip,
pedals flashing like a shooting star.
Coasting like a sled on snow,
as free as a bumble bee.
Zooming around like a fighter jet.
Bicycling is me!

Bicycle Dreams

by Michael Salinger

My wheels are spinning,
pedals are turning,
hands on the handlebars.
As I roll along,
training wheels gone,
a bike riding superstar.
My thumb rings the bell,
as I speed down the block,
wind whooshes through my hair.
I love riding my bike
'cause it makes me feel
like I can go anywhere.

Inside

Inside Win

by Michael Salinger

This time my win is quiet,
so almost no one knows.
My victory I keep inside
like roller coaster elbows.

I faced up to a fear
that was personal and mine,
and this time came out ahead
at an invisible finish line.

Ordinary

by Sara Holbrook

What if I'm never rich
or a princess,
or a king?
What if I never am an astronaut
or quarterback a team?
I love to dream.

But if I never am a rock star
or don't grow up Ivy League;
if I never go to State
or read my name on a marquee –
If I don't have my say on talk shows
or have cards marked "CEO,"
thank my mom in front of
thousands,
play Olympic,
bring home gold;
what dreams will picture
when I sleep?
What is the label that I'll carry?

How will I know if I succeed?
Where is the glory in ordinary?

My Official List

by Sara Holbrook

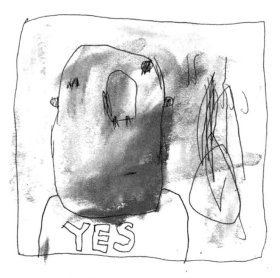

Candy hearts.
Soaring kites.
Chasing.
Saving.
Marching bands.
Movies that might bring a tear.
Roller coasters.
Knowing what it's all about.
Pizzas.
Climbing trees.
A light spring breeze.
Anticipation.
Dressing up.
Growing up.
Getting presents.

Author's note: Read across.

Poison darts.
Mosquito bites.
Chased.
Waste.
Slimy hands.
Guitar solos that last a year.
Collared shirts and Brussel sprouts.
Divas.
Stains on knees.
A sniffling sneeze.
Running late.
A fashion plate.
Growing old.
Getting told
    and aqua.

Ask why this is and always was?
My answer is, *just because.*

Hungry

by Michael Salinger

I am
Belly grumbling
Lip licking
Refrigerator looking
Tummy aching
Food sniffing
Crumb gathering
Grumpy feeling
Cookie begging
Cake wanting
Donut craving
Ice cream wishing
Candy dishing
Hungry
And can't you see
Why I hesitate?
There's nothing but vegetables
On my plate!

Thinking Small

by Sara Holbrook

The careless
    shoulder shrug.
Throat tickles
    in the night.
Eyes
    that drift astray.
A shadow
    standing in my light.
Friends playing games
    instead of talking.
Forks
    scraped between closed teeth.
Phony smiles.
Clothes in piles.
Unmatched socks.
Ticking clocks.
Searching
    for lost keys.
Little things
    that make my teeth itch.
Metaphoric fleas.

Lost Hope

by Sara Holbrook

Don't shrug
'cause that's the way it goes.
I want it back.
Where did it go?
That run-away,
Lost Hope.

Chased off by
Could-have-beens
that won't?

Networking

by Sara Holbrook

I flip through status updates
for the day, and think I'm
feeling. . . just okay,
then emoji shop:
glad, impressed, excited, angry, blue,
researching an attitude.
I copy/post an image
snagged online for free,
quickly, lest some darker
mood grabs a hold of me.

The Ride

by Sara Holbrook

After you've climbed the hill
to see the view,
then slid down the other side –
after you've skinned both knees,
broken bones,
and cracked your helmet twice –
after you've tasted the rush
of passing through
in front, behind, beside –
what choice is there
but to climb back up,
pump the pedals, and ride?

Bad Joke

by Sara Holbrook

Glasses and braces?
Is this some bad joke?
A conspiracy
so I look like a dope?
Plastic bug eyes
and tinsel buck teeth.
What did I do
to deserve this grief?

Why can't I feel normal?
Why can't I feel good?
I'm hopeless
and helpless and
misunderstood.
I can't stand this age,
and it's just my luck …
I'll turn out to be bald
when I finally grow up.

Digestion

by Michael Salinger

We have a mouth where the food goes in.
The pharynx decides which path it should take.
Down the esophagus munchies pass,
peristalsis pushing and squeezing
chewed up goo into the stomach.
Mixing with acids and enzymes (and a little gas)
for a bit of time.
Then into the small intestines
where the bloodstream receives a nutrient injection.
Once we've squeezed all the good stuff out
we visit my large intestine where
compacted waste is sent for collection.
Then it's stored in my rectum
and when the time is right
it's expelled through my anus.
What's for dinner tonight?

What a Brain!

by Sara Holbrook

Inside my skull, between my ears,
are my gut feelings, hopes and fears.
It's nerve central!
My bossy brain
that makes me "ouch"
when I feel pain.
It tells me when I'm hungry, tired,
shocked, excited,
lazy, wired.
Its stem heads up my bony spine,
and paired up with that power line
it blinks my eyes and moves my feet,
and gives my heart a steady beat.

My brain's the boss!
So if I act a little bit insane?
Don't blame me.
Blame the brain.

Outreach?

by Sara Holbrook

All alone?
Or telephone?
In-reach?
Outreach?
Which?
And if I choose,
how long before
I change my mind
and switch?
My brain's too full.
I can't converse,
but isolation's so
much worse.
Opt in?
Opt out?
What comes next?
Guess
I could (maybe) text.

Home

Blueprints

by Sara Holbrook

Will my ears grow long as Grandpa's?
What makes us look like kin?
Tell me where'd I get long eyelashes
and where'd I get my chin?

Where'd I get my ice cream sweet tooth
and this nose that wiggles when I talk?
Where'd I get my dizzy daydreams
and my foot-rolling, side-step walk?

Did I inherit my sense of humor
and these crooked, ugly toes?
What if I balloon like Uncle Harry
and have to shave my nose?

How long after I start growing
until I start to shrink?
Am I going to lose my teeth
some day?
My hair?
My mind?
Do you think
I'll be tall or short or thin
or bursting at the seams?
Am I naturally this crazy?
Is it something in my genes?

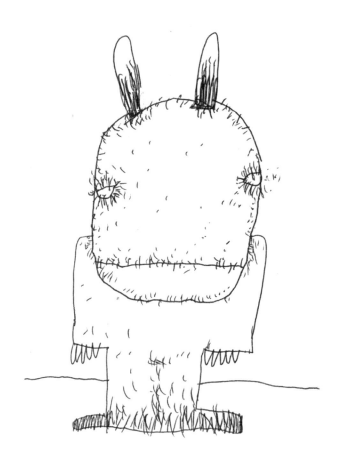

I'm more than
who I am,
I'm also
who I'm from.
It's a scary speculation –
Who will I become?

My Noisy Family

by *Michael Salinger*

When my family gets together
It can be very loud
Even when he's not mad
My grandpa shouts
The TV's always going in the next room
I can never be heard in this crowd
Nobody laughs bigger than dad
And the dog is barking 'cause he wants out
My big brother stomps his feet boom boom boom
And my baby sister cries louder than thunder
My grandma and I - we just wonder
Who's going to do the dishes?

Upholding Myself

by Sara Holbrook

I'm going to build an airbase
in that singing pine,
climb the ladder limbs
and leave this angry war behind.

No doubt,
they'll call for reinforcements
when they realize I am gone.
But my ambitions are as high
as my survival instinct's
strong.

This warfare will continue,
with me caught up in the combat
or daydreaming up above.
I'll wait there for
the treaty terms.

I'm holding out
for love.

Nearly Distant

by Sara Holbrook

Families,
kitchen magnets,
repel each time
they turn their backs.
Distancing themselves
when they should
listen,
not react.

Socks!

by Sara Holbrook

Socks on the table.
Socks in my drawer.
Socks in my pocket.
Socks on the floor.
Socks in my backpack.
Socks left in jeans.
Socks lost in cars.
Socks in my dreams.
Socks draped from doors.
Socks stuffed in chairs.
Socks beneath,
between,
and everywhere.
Why can't I find
a single pair?

Crazed

by Sara Holbrook

Zoom.
Zip.
Hurry.
Slip.
Razzle.
Frazzle.
Hurry.
Trip.
Whiz.
Wheeze.
Feet ablaze.
Hurry!
Hurry!
Late!
Crazed!

I'm Here

by Sara Holbrook

Too much slack in my strings,
        I can't move.
I'm flopped in my footprints,
too loose in the arms to light a fuse
or feel my way out.
        DON'T SHOUT!
        I know.
I've gone blank in the face.
Black in the eye.
        I know.
I'm not keeping pace.
Knee deep in this muck,
        No, I can't hurry up.
                I'm stuck.

Take on Saturday

by Michael Salinger

What's it gonna take
    for me to wake
up on a Saturday?

What's it gonna take
    for me to shake
sleep from my head today?

What's it gonna take
    for my belly ache
to finally go away?

It's gonna take
    a pancake.
It's gonna take
    a pancake.
It's gonna take
    a pancake.

Grill me up
a big ol' stack
and I will be
okay!

Fishing

by Michael Salinger

I like to go fishing with my dad.
We sit super quiet and wait.
We watch the bobber float on the water
hoping a fish will take the bait.
It's a special time for him and me,
out on the water just us two,
and even if they all get away,
it's still one of my favorite things to do.

A River Washing

by Sara Holbrook

That old river
whispers in my right ear
to sluice through my head,
turning rocks to pebbles,
and pebbles into sand.
Then it burbles out the left ear,
leaving me refreshed.
The river does all the work.
All I have to do is stand.

Fishing for Bargains

by Michael Salinger

I bought a rod
and I bought a reel.
I bought some lures
and a brand-new creel.
I bought some waders.
I bought a vest.
I bought a tackle box
and all the rest
of the stuff I need
to go out and catch
some fish for free.

The Hardware Store

by Michael Salinger

Hammer
Hammer
Hammer
Hammer
Hammer
Hammer
Drill
All purpose
Heavy duty
Wood filler, roto tiller, screws
Saw blades, wing nuts, steel toed shoes
Half off
Items on this shelf
Do it
Do it
Do it
Do it
Do it yourself.

Levers

by Michael Salinger

A screwdriver
opening a big can of paint
is a machine
that's simple and clever.
Place a beam
on a fulcrum
distributing force –
Presto!
You've made yourself a lever.

Gears

by Michael Salinger

A gear is a simple machine
because it only needs two parts.
Like wheels with teeth,
when one spins the other starts
to turn in what is called a ratio.
Gears come in all different shapes and sizes
mostly doing their work inside of stuff.
Where may we use some gears today?
What spins or turns?
What rotates or grinds?
What lifts or what lowers?
How many gears can you find?

Pairs

by Sara Holbrook

Parents are like mittens,
supposed to come in pairs,
and when they come in singles
it really isn't fair.

Would you be satisfied
with buying single socks?
Or settle for one hand
mounted on a clock?

Can't life be more like shopping,
where all the shoes have mates?
You pick out what you want,
and return stuff when it breaks?

Some Families

by Sara Holbrook

Some families are extended
with grandmothers and aunts,
with cousins by the dozens.
No one has a chance
to say which ones they choose
and which they want removed.
'Cause family's what they got,
a little or a lot.
Some families start small
counting fingers while they grow,
others simply shrink
or take off for the coast.
Some families get divided
and then get rearranged.
When grown-ups choose new partners,
the family dance gets strange.
Some people think the family thing
is mostly overrated.
Some people feel left out,
and some stay isolated.
Some people pick each other,
and who knows who's behind it;
they bunch up like bouquets,
and family's where they find it.

Berate

by Michael Salinger

Berate should be handing out earplugs
his lecturing tends to get loud
his criticisms long and severe
he means to demean, that's clear
he tends to go over the top
shouting and scolding with zest
making his victim feel small
is the one of the things he does best
needless to say, his friends are far
and few
which just may explain
a thing or two.

A Breather

by Sara Holbrook

When you ...
Then I ...
Then you ...
Then I ...
Anger jumps between us
like a wind-blown forest fire.
We fight,
throwing every word we have
in the turbulence
with merciless intent.
The crazy,
frenzied,
fury burns
until there's almost nothing left.

Time to take a breath.

How to Walk Around the Block

by Michael Salinger

Wear shoes.
If they have laces, make sure they are tied.
Pick a direction and go.
Double foot hop
over sidewalk cracks,
then stop and pick up a rock.
No snooping in your neighbor's mailbox,
(You'll get in trouble if you get caught.)
Woof bark woof bark woof bark woof;
ask before you pet that dog.
That stick could use a new location.
Remember,
where you started is your destination.
'Cause 'round the block
is a circle
(even if it's really a square).
Arriving back at your front door,
you'll be a different person
when you get there.

Critters

Dog Logic

by Sara Holbrook

It's a contract.
Humans work.
They shop.
They prepare the food.
In exchange
I nap
and bark at the mailman.
Fetching's extra.
Depends on
my mood.

Smartest Dog in the World

by Michael Salinger

My dog is really super smart.
I've taught her everything she knows.
She rings a bell on the front door,
I stop, and let her out to go.
When it's her dinnertime
she brings me her empty bowl.
I fill it with her favorite food,
she dances on her toes.
When it's time to go to sleep,
she leads me to my bed.
Snuggled together under the covers,
I close my eyes and begin to see
maybe I have not trained her -
maybe she's trained me.

Self Esteem?

by Sara Holbrook

I tell my dog he's bad.
I laugh when he jumps and misses.
I gag when he drinks from the toilet,
and then tries to give me kisses.
I mock the way he twitches his nose,
and sometimes he makes me scream.
His nicknames are *Stinky* and *Hairball*.

Can dogs get low self-esteem?

Roos

by Michael Salinger

Kangaroos
have a knack,
jumping and kicking,
you would think
their knees are made of springs.
They wear a front facing backpack
as they bounce across the outback,
keeping busy
knocking around
and thinking marsupial things.

Happiness Comes Hopping

by Sara Holbrook

Happiness comes hopping
when work is finished
or,
it brightens up my windows
and rattles at my door,
with news that something's
coming.
Excitement's standing near.

Its hop-hop-happy hopping
jumps right over
doubt and fear.

And though
I know its goofy,
if I watch it for a while,
that hop-hop-happy hopping
always makes me smile.

Monkeyshines

by Michael Salinger

Do not feed the monkey!
Don't look him in the eye.
Don't smile,
even if you're happy.
Let me tell you why.
Monkeys are greedy
and bad company.
One treat won't satisfy.
If you feed the monkey,
monkeys are not shy.
They reach into your pockets,
pry your glasses
from your eyes.
They've got sticky little fingers.
You can kiss your bananas goodbye.
Do not feed the monkey.
Don't look him in the eye.

When a Possum Grins

by Michael Salinger

When a possum grins,
shows his thorny teeth,
though he's trying to be friendly
and means no harm,
he still appears pretty scary.
It's not his fault.
It's just how he looks.
He was born scraggly and hairy
with warped whiskers,
twisted ears,
and a tail that's long, bald, and pointy.
It's no big wonder
he makes us flinch and shudder.
Who could love
such an ugly thing
besides
the possum's mother?

Bats!

by Sara Holbrook and Michael Salinger

Nocturnal
   as a lightning bug.
Hanging like a tree fruit.
Beeping like a
   smoke detector.
Fuzzy as a hamster.
Face like a free-dried dog.
Tracking like a sonar.
Flapping like a
   novice in the deep end.
Mega bat is me.

Nocturnal

by Michael Salinger

I went to bed hours ago.
I'm supposed to be snoozing.
But I'm glowing under my covers,
internet cruising.
I'm chatting with my friends,
watching music videos,
shooting zombies in the head,
earbuds in, so no one knows.
At night nobody is telling me
to put my phone away.
I guess I'm sort of nocturnal,
I can sleep during the day.

Squiggles

by Michael Salinger

I caught some squiggles in the pond
and put them in a big jar.
I gave them bits of lettuce to eat,
'cause they looked kinda starved.
They began to grow real fat,
and as their bodies spread,
legs popped out of their sides,
and eyes bulged from their heads.
Their squiggle tails disappeared.
They were no longer polliwogs.
My squiggles they are all gone.
Now what am I gonna do with these noisy frogs?

Peeping from Under the Covers

by Sara Holbrook

Peepers peeping
announce that spring has come.
In shrill choruses and monologues,
from banks of streams, perched on logs,
they sing of season's turnabout,
"Stop your hibernating!"
They call me out.
Brown and green,
without a word,
mostly unseen,
but not unheard.

Coming Soon

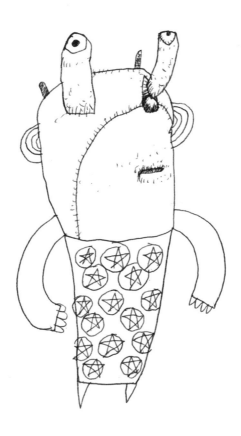

My Identity Kit

by Michael Salinger

I don't throw my tee shirts away
just because they got a few holes.
I don't throw my tee shirts away
if they have a stain or two.
I don't throw my tee shirts away
when they're stretched out a bit.
They don't even have to fit
just right.
I don't throw my tee shirts away,
at least not without a fight.
It's not something I do.
I mean, I just refuse.
My tee shirts speak for me
better than my shoes.

Checkups

by Sara Holbrook

A friendship should
have checkups –
pressures,
weights,
temperatures,
eyes and ears –
before it starves,
overextends, or
breaks down
in a terminal
case of tears.

What's Just

by Sara Holbrook

Just deny.
Just postpone.
Just press forward, *just* delete.
      Didn't see it.
      Not my mix.
      Couldn't care.
      Cannot fix.
So whatever.
I'm *just* so not into this.

Except . . .
      Just some sweat on my forehead,
      just this bite on my lip.
Except . . .
      Just this clench in my eyebrows,
      just this scream in my throat.
I should *just* walk away.
This is *just* not my fight.

Except . . .
      My voice *just* escaped,
      and I *just* have to say
that
that
just isn't right.

Sometimes...

by Michael Salinger

There's a little guy sitting on my shoulder
who likes to give advice.
Sometimes it's good.
Sometimes it's bad.
Sometimes it's mean.
Sometimes it's nice.
Sometimes I listen.
Sometimes I don't.
Sometimes I wish he'd leave.
And sometimes I have to admit
the little guy is me.

Feelings Make Me Real

by Sara Holbrook

You are not the boss of me,
And what I feel inside.
Please don't say, "Let's see a smile,"
Or ask me not to cry.

I am not too sensitive –
You think my inside's steel?
You can't tell me how to be.
Feelings make me real.

Why Not?

by Sara Holbrook

Why not?
Can't we talk it over?
Isn't there another way?
You thought it was a great idea
just the other day.

I feel like something died.
I feel you kinda lied.
I wish we could have tried.
That's all I have to say.

Except . . .

Sorry

by Sara Holbrook

Sorry
follows like my shadow,
fastened at the heels.
It trails me to my room
and sits with me at meals.

It nags me in my dreams
when I have gone to bed.
That Sorry pest hangs on
until
it's finally said.

You, Too?

by Sara Holbrook

Whispers by lockers.
Whispers in throats.
Undercurrents.
Gossip.
Rumors.
Snapchats.
Jokes.
Bobbing along
in this babbling brook,
hoping I won't
get sunk by a
random comment,
eye roll, or look.
Wobbling along
in this narrow canoe,
just hanging on.
It's hard to believe
that others
are, too.

Labels

by Sara Holbrook

People get tagged with these labels,
like African-American,
Native-American,
White,
Asian, Hispanic,
or Euro-Caucasian –
I just ask that you get my name right.
I'm part Willie,
part Ethel,
part Suzi and Scott.
Part assembly-line worker,
part barber, a lot of dancer
and salesman. Part grocer and mailman.
Part rural, part city, part cook
and part caveman.
I'm a chunk-style vegetable soup
of cultural little bits,
my recipe's unique
and no one label fits.
Grouping folks together
is an individual waste.
You can't know me by just a look,
you have to take a taste.

Together?

by Sara Holbrook

Not known for being delicate,
obedient,
or sweet,
but proud to poke
through sidewalk cracks
bright against the gray,
dancing in a city lot
or tucked beneath a tree –
If I were a dandelion
would you stand with me?

Love Heals

by Sara Holbrook

Across oceans, miles, the street,
around the corner
with my grandma
      we share smiles.
After random pushes, pokes, and poundings,
beyond a world of scornful meanness,
through her weathered door
      I stumble.
Without any major effort,
over bruises blue and black,
into my fractured spirit
      she pours glue --
across, within, and through.

Loves me, Loves me Not

by Sara Holbrook

Roses?
So sweet,
but little to say.
Dandelions
fluff and
fly away.
Daffodils bloom after
crocuses spring
from quiet
banks of snow.
Each tulip has
a velvet heart,
but only summer's
daisies
promise the absolute truth
when they
are
torn
a
  p
   a
    r
     t.

Grown-ups

by Sara Holbrook

I can't do
until they let me.
If I do,
that's when they get me.

I have to ask.
They get to tell.
I must keep still.
They get to yell.

Sometimes they say yes,
and then they refuse.
Then I get to plead,
and they get to choose.
And sometimes I win.
And sometimes I lose.

Quiet Questions

by Sara Holbrook

Quiet questions
sneak around,
squinching up the eyes.
They shift in chairs,
bite on nails,
and let out little sighs.
Quizzically,
with tilted heads,
they often stand and stare,
both hands propped on hips.
Quiet questions
sneak around
before they reach the lips.

Out of the Box

by Michael Salinger

Relax!
This thing may have four sides,
but there's an exit at the top.
Extinguish your anxiety
by expanding your reality.
Turn the dial of doubt
from MAX to min.
Flex your muscles,
jump out and in
to new expanses.
Try interpretive dances!
Learn to play the sax!
Perform a high wire act!
Don't just be a fixture.
Join the social mixture.
Imagine the extraordinary
adventures
you will find.
A box is just
a state of mind.

The Sound of Alone

by Sara Holbrook

No need to speak,
smile,
or comb.
Quiet thoughts whisper.
I cup my ear,
leaning in.
Listen!
The sound of
Alone.

Shopping

by Sara Holbrook

Would this sweater make me popular?
Make my teeth straight?
Bring me joy?
Would I be famous in the hallway?
Could it help attract a boy?
Will this sweater make me skinny?
Tall? Exceptionally brave?
Would it text me when I'm lonely?
Or make my hair behave?
Should I borrow from my mom
or borrow from the store?
Put this thing on credit?
Would this sweater make me more
than who I am?
Hanger in my hand,
I eye my future debt,
weighing what I want
against
what I'll really get.

Just Wait

by Sara Holbrook

You see nothing.
Nobody.
A shy sun
being crowded out
by a crush of east bound clouds.
But inside snare drums march in my ears,
I can't control my bouncing knee.
I'm a grizzly roar
that's been caged for – years.
My leaping thoughts are ping pong balls.
My eyes keep rubbering 'round.
I'm not some dusty relic,
a fossil,
waiting to be found.
There's fire in me,
a singular power.
A beanstalk ready to climb.
I'm buds on the tree,
a seed in the ground.
Just wait.
I'm biding my time.

Victory

by Michael Salinger

Victory
doesn't have to be loud,
a canon erupting in the night.

Victory
needn't gloat
because it won the fight.

Victory
can be proud,
peaceful, and serene,
offering a handshake
to the other team.

Victory
doesn't have to beat its chest
talkin' trash,
or make a splash
to prove that it's the best.

Victory
doesn't have to be
so all up in your face.
In fact,

Victory
tastes most excellent
mixed with a
tablespoon of grace.

Lights Out

by Sara Holbrook

I'm tucked in bed
except my head
runs like a broken toilet.

Still wired from caffeine
and that blinking screen,
my brain's wound and I can't uncoil it.

Crouching, panting, head spinning around,
like a virtual hero covering ground –
I press pause and take a breath.

Perhaps the flashing lights will disappear
If I close both eyes and jiggle my ear.
The real me needs some rest.

Coming Soon

by Sara Holbrook

I am how I act
and
I am what I eat.
I sometimes react,
and
I'm not yet complete.

Nothing about me is permanent.
Growing up
is a chain reaction.
The mirror may reflect
"ugly duckling,"
but inside I'm a
"coming attraction."

Scott Pickering is an artist/musician living and working in Cleveland, OH. His playful, brightly colored drawings can be seen locally, nationally, and internationally. His spontaneous doodles can be found on building and in galleries.
You can find him at Pufftube1 on Instagram

Sara Holbrook is the author of poetry for children and adults as well as educational texts for teachers. She frequently visits schools and speaks at teacher conferences all over the world. Her middle grade novel, *The Enemy, Detroit 1954* won the 2018 Jane Addams Peace Award. She is from Mentor, OH, where she lives with Michael, two dogs and one needy cat.
@saraholbrook | www.saraholbrook.com

Michael Salinger is a father, author, cyclist, fisherman, educator and world traveler. After 23 years in manufacturing, he transitioned to a life of helping students and teachers find their voices. His books include poetry for adults and kids. His newest teacher book, *From Striving to Thriving Writers, Strategies to Jump-Start Writing* is a collaboration with Sara and Stephanie Harvey.
@michaelsalinger| www.outspokenlit.com